SPEAKING SHADOWS

ECHOES FROM THE SILENT CORNERS

VOLUME 1

SATISH PUTHRAN
TANZEELA NAUSHEEN
TAHREEM NOOR
MANSI BHAGWATE
PRAPTI KADAM
SAI MALLAREDDY

SATISH PUTHRAN
SPEAKING SHADOWS
ECHOES FROM THE SILENT CORNERS

SPEAKING SHADOWS

ECHOES FROM THE SILENT CORNERS - VOLUME 1

First Edition Version 1.0

Cover Design By : Tanzeela Nausheen / Tahreem Noor Hassan / Mansi Bhagwate
Printed In : India
Published By : Satish Puthran

SPEAKING SHADOWS

SATISH PUTHRAN
SPEAKING SHADOWS
ECHOES FROM THE SILENT CORNERS

EPIGRAPH

"In the hush of unspoken words, stories find their voice. Shadows do not merely follow us—they remember, they whisper, they dream."
— Speaking Shadows

DEDICATION

Dedicated to the unknown writers whose stories carry the weight of emotions untold, may your words illuminate paths and inspire hearts on this shared journey of the human spirit.

For every aspiring writer who believed in their story, even when the world didn't know their name—this anthology is a celebration of your voice, your truth, and your heart.

PREFACE

A collection of voices by unknown writers, bound together by words, but each uniquely distinct in its approach. In these pages, you'll encounter a tapestry of experiences—some familiar, others thought-provokingly strange—but all woven together with a common thread: the power of storytelling. As you read, I invite you to reflect on the shared human condition, the beauty of differences, and the truth that in every narrative, there's something we can all find within ourselves. We can relate to or resonate with their words.

It's a celebration of your voice, your truth, and your heart. Let the whole universe hear your voices—make it loud.

SATISH PUTHRAN
SPEAKING SHADOWS
ECHOES FROM THE SILENT CORNERS

AN UNEXPECTED CHAPTER

I wasn't supposed to be here.

At least, that's what I thought.

When I submitted my piece, I was just another name on a list, another voice among voices. I didn't know the other writers, their stories, or how my words would fit into this book. I only knew one thing—I had something to say.

And maybe that's all that matters. Because stories, just like people, have a way of finding where they belong. And somehow, mine found its way here—between these pages, among these voices, and now, in your hands.

For the longest time, I was told that my love for English was something to be mocked. That speaking fluently made me 'too much,' that my passion for words made me different in a way that wasn't always welcomed. I was called names, judged for simply enjoying the language I felt most at home in. Some people made me feel as though my love for literature was something unnatural, something that set me apart in a way I didn't ask for.

But literature became my escape, my voice, my proof that I had something to say, no matter who tried to silence it.

And now, to share a book with such incredible writers—people who see the world through words just as I do—is a moment I never expected but will always be grateful for.

So as you turn these pages, some words will resonate, some will stay with you, and some might even change the way you see the world. And maybe—just maybe—one of them will be mine.

But more than anything, I am deeply grateful. To be able to share space with these incredible writers—people who have walked ahead of me, whose words carry the weight of experience and the depth of literature—is a privilege beyond words. Their perspectives, their artistry, their wisdom—this book holds more than just stories; it holds pieces of minds that shape the world.

And as for me? I am writing this in the middle of my Class 10 board exams, right between struggling with math formulas and dreaming about words that refused to stay unwritten. But if there's one thing I know, it's that literature finds its way through everything. Literature has the power to heal anything and everything, and to every reader flipping through these pages, supporting these artistic souls—thank you. The world needs more of you.

Moreover, And a heartfelt thank you to Author Satish Puthran for giving me the opportunity to be a part of this incredible journey. Your belief in the power of words and in voices like mine means more than I can express. This book is not just a collection of stories—it's a testament to the artistry and passion you've brought together.

With gratitude,

© Tahreem Noor

INDEX

SATISH PUTHRAN

SPEAKING SHADOWS

ECHOES FROM THE SILENT CORNERS

ACKNOWLEDGMENTS

|| ॐ गणेशाय नमः ||

|| ॐ सरस्वती नमो नमः ||

We extend our heartfelt gratitude to everyone who contributed to Speaking Shadows: : Echoes from the Silent Corners.

Special thanks to our readers for embracing these voices, our families for their unwavering support, and all those who find meaning in the silent echoes of storytelling.

— Satish Puthran

INTRODUCTION

In the quietest corners of our minds, where unspoken words linger and emotions take refuge, shadows speak. They whisper of longing, of memories etched in time, of dreams nurtured in silence. *Speaking Shadows: Echoes from the Silent Corners* is a collection of reflections, musings, and unfiltered thoughts that give voice to these hushed emotions.

Each piece in this anthology is a fragment of the human experience—some radiant with hope, others heavy with solitude, yet all resonating with the universal truth of what it means to feel, to remember, and to dream. Through poetry, prose, and introspective narratives, this book invites you to explore the depths of emotions often left unsaid.

Let these echoes from the silent corners remind you that even in the quietest moments, thoughts have the power to speak, and shadows have stories to tell.

PARTICIPATING AUTHORS

Tarun Khatnani

Anshita Rai

Arjun Malhotra

Shruti Bangarwar

Rojith RJ

Vanisha Rai

Tata Mahesh Chaudhary

Tahreem Noor Hassan

Tanzeela Nausheen

Yuganshi Raj

Mansi Bhagwate

Simran Sahoo

Supriya Sharma

Sai Mallareddy

V Heymonth Kumar

Akshay R Rao

Mayu Kadam

Namrata Singh

Preeti Gujar

Shabnam Jalal

Killada Shreevani

Magie Gadidesi

Deepa Vasant Shenoy

Deep Thinker

Rajat Kumar Dalai

Rahul Jhawar

Ashrin Mathew

Smt. Mugdha Rane

Smt. Vijayashree Thorave

Rangeesh Chandrasekar

Kunal Joshi

Rachel Raju Alice

Joel

Ashna Rose Tharian

Abirami Aji

Prapti Kadam

Dhananjay Gupta

Priyanshu Kumar

Monish Shetty

Komal Gupta

Adarsh Anand

BIO OF FEW PARTICIPATING AUTHORS

SATISH PUTHRAN
SPEAKING SHADOWS
ECHOES FROM THE SILENT CORNERS

TANZEELA NAUSHEEN

Tanzeela Nausheen, born on November 2nd, is an Electronics Engineer by profession. She has worked in multinational companies as well as in academia as a lecturer. Beyond her professional career, she is deeply passionate about animal welfare and actively works to spread awareness about them. She is also dedicated to environmental causes, particularly in waste segregation.

Writing has always been a part of Tanzeela's journey. She is a passionate writer of short stories and reflective thoughts, drawing inspiration from her own experiences. From a young age, she found solace in expressing herself through words, keeping a diary where she documented her daily life, emotions, and even song lyrics that she memorized. At the time, she didn't fully understand why she wrote, but she loved the process of putting her feelings into words.

Her journey as a writer took a significant turn when she discovered Satish Puthran, who was helping aspiring writers. This opportunity allowed her to share her short stories and thoughts, uncovering a hidden talent she hadn't fully explored before. Despite facing difficult times, she never gave up on herself. Writing became her way of healing, and now she hopes to support others going through similar struggles.

With a deep understanding of life and resilience, Tanzeela continues to write, inspire, and contribute to the causes she believes in, striving to make a meaningful impact through her words and actions.

AUTHOR TAHREEM NOOR

Tahreem Noor was born on the 27th of November. She is a passionate writer with a penchant for storytelling. She published her first book "The Shimmering Moon" on 15th Feb 2024. She developed a deep love for English Literature ever since she was a kid. Her hobbies, mainly revolve around being creative and unique in her way possible. Tahreem is a straightforward person and she likes to take pride in her work. For a long time, She was demotivated but never gave up on her Passion. She looks at this endeavor as just one small step in a long journey of penning many pages in the years to come...

While Tahreem is recognized for her exceptional skills as an author, it's worth noting that her talents extend beyond the realm of writing. In addition to being a professional author, Tahreem Noor is also a captivating and insightful anchor.

Those readers who wish to buy can order her poetry book 'The Shimmering Moon' copy from https://notionpress.com/in/read/the-shimmering-moon/ & support her future journey.

➡ Readers she is a published author — though she haven't sold many copies, she managed to sell over 25 books independently, without any guidance, & none of those sales were from friends or family. She is also a professional anchor & have hosted a show, plus she hold leadership roles in her school as the Cultural Secretary & the English Club Prefect.

SATISH PUTHRAN
SPEAKING SHADOWS
ECHOES FROM THE SILENT CORNERS

MANSI BHAGWATE

Mansi Bhagwate is a first year MFA student at Drexel University. Previously, she was from Mumbai, India and moved to the US to pursue a Master's degree in Occupational Therapy.

Mansi writes in various genres including fiction and creative non-fiction and has been published by Beyond Words Literary Magazine, Apiary Magazine, Short Fiction Break and Tenderly Magazine. She has also written two short films in her native language Marathi, one of which (Chaha Biscuit) was showcased at the Kerala short film festival. She was a semi-finalist at America's Next Great Author, a reality television show about writers. She likes to examine the intersection of animals, humans and the environment in her writing. She also likes to write about cultural intersections and assimilating as an immigrant in the United States.

| मुझ में तू |

यह सोचना भी कितना सुख देता है की जो चीज़ें घटी हैं वह उसी क्रम ना घटी होती तो आज वर्तमान कितना अलग होता और कितना अलग होता तुम्हारा और मेरा साथ। दुःख पहाड़ों सा होता है जितना ऊँचा होता है उतना ही गहरा भी, सुख नदियों सा बहता चला जाता है। मैं ख़ुद को पहाड़ों में महसूस करता हूँ और उनके बीच से निकलने वाली नदी की तलाश कर रहा हूँ।

पिछले कुछ महीने ना जाने किस चीज़ की बेचैनी में बीते हैं, शायद यह कुछ लिखने की भूख थी जो सता रही थी या फिर मेरी क़लम जिसने मेरा बहुत इंतज़ार किया है। यह लेख इसी इंतज़ार का फल है।

मैं बहुत बात करने वाला इंसान हूँ इसीलिए मैं अपनी हर कहानी को बोल देना चाहता हूँ या लिख देना चाहता हूँ।

कुछ भी लिखते वक़्त मेरे मन में अजीब से चित्र बनते हैं। यह चित्र विकृत हैं, मैं इन्हें एक साथ जोड़ कर एक ही तस्वीर में नहीं रख पाता जिससे मेरा मन अशांत रहता है

और फिर मैं किसी चीज़ के चले जाने के बारे में सोचने लगता हूँ।

चले जाना !

अजीब होता है ना?

मौसम का चले जाना,

मन का चले जाना,

इंसान का चले जाना,

विश्वास का चले जाना,

प्रेम का चले जाना।

त्रासदी यह है की इन सब के चले जाने के बाद भी इनका कुछ हिस्सा छूट जाता है जो भीतर घर कर लेता है। मेरे भीतर शायद तुम हो, तुम्हारा प्रेम है और मेरा विश्वास है। इसी घर में किसी रोज़ तुम मेरे क़रीब हुआ करती थी। सर्द हवाओं वाले दिन तुम अपना हाथ मेरे हाथों की उंगलियों में फँसा लेती थी और हर पल मेरे पास रहती थी पर अब इन्हीं हाथों के छूट जाने की पीड़ा रह गई है। इसमें से सुख

की धूप जा चुकी है। तुम्हारा यही घर अब मेरे अशांत मन में टूटा हुआ सा दिखाई पड़ता है।

मेरे लिये हर रास्ता अब खाली हो गया है अब इन पर सिर्फ़ मुझे चलना है। इस अकेले चलने की प्रक्रिया में मैं ख़ुद को बहुत महसूस करता हूँ और जो भीतर तंग कर रहा होता है उसे बड़बड़ाता हूँ। दिन बदलते रहते हैं, शामें ठहरती नहीं है पर रास्ते अब भी वहीं है और मेरी हर टीस इसी रास्ते के सफ़र से जुड़ी है किंतु मुझे सुख भी इन्हीं पर चलते रहने से मिलता है। मैं कहीं पर भी जल्दी से नहीं पहुँचना चाहता था इसीलिए कभी कोई छोटा रास्ता नहीं लेता था। तुम्हारे साथ तो मेरा सफ़र छोटा ही रह गया है और अब इस लंबे रास्ते की रंगीन शाम में बस श्वेत सा मैं रह गया हूँ। सफ़र अपनी मंज़िल आने पर ख़त्म हो जाता है पर रास्ता अभी बहुत लम्बा है और इस पर तुम और मैं अपनी दिशाओं में काफ़ी दूर जा चुके हैं।

मैं लिखना बहुत महत्वपूर्ण समझता हूँ। जिसे मैं बयाँ नहीं कर सकता उसे मैं कागज़ पर उतार कर उसे पीला होने के लिये छोड़ देता हूँ। मेरे शब्द जो उस रोज़ मैं कह नहीं पाया

था, मेरी भेद्यता जिसे मैं किसी के सामने ला नहीं पाया था आज पन्नो में कैद करता जाता हूँ।

तुम्हें लिखता हूँ तो तुम और ख़ूबसूरत दिखने लगती हो। मुझे समझ नहीं आता की मेरे शब्द तुम्हें इतना ख़ूबसूरत बना रहे हैं या तुम इन्हें या यह महज़ मेरी कल्पना है।

मैं जब जब लिखने की ओर बढ़ता हूँ और सब कुछ शब्दों में पिरो देने के बाद अंत तक पहुँच जाता हूँ तब मुझे यह अजीब सा डर होता है की यह लेख भी यहीं ख़त्म हो जाएगा। आखिर क्यों मैं इसमें कुछ और शब्द नहीं जोड़ सकता? या फिर क्यों नहीं मैं अपनी भेद्यता को इसमें पूरी तरह से झिंझोड़ देता? मेरा ख़ुदसे यही सवाल करना इस आलेख का अंत है और तुम्हारा चित्र भी इन्हीं सवालों के साथ मेरे मन में पूरा बन उठा था, जिसे मैं मेरे जवाबों के साथ फिर से तोड़ना नहीं चाहता था। इससे बेहतर अंत नहीं हो सकता क्योंकि अब इसमें तुम हो, एक टूटा हुआ सा घर है, कुछ पन्ने हैं, मेरा प्रेम और मेरे वही अधूरे सवाल।

© तरुण खटनानी 'मधुप'

इंतज़ार तुम्हारा

झरोके पर बैठकर... पुराने गीतों को सुनकर

मन कुछ बहक गया है...

आज शाम ज्यादा अपनी सी लगती है

मानो मेरी बातें बिना कहे समझ रही है...

ख्यालों में कोई है...

एहसास है...

उसका ख्वाब है

बस झलक नहीं दिखती....

चेहरे पर मुस्कान है उसके इंतज़ार की....

इंतज़ार फिर ऐसी ही शाम की...

पर इस बार एहसास नही, मौजूदगी की..!!

© अंशिता राय

HOPEFUL OPTIMIST

I've been hurt and broken a lot too many times,

I wanna stay in those moments which just let me smile.

Never been one to speak my mind,

I am just happy being with people who accept my viles.

It's the feelings in my heart I never speak aloud,

It's the hopeless romanticism which never crosses bounds.

Unnecessary screaming, internal bouts,

And it's the darkened demons which always hound.

Running away, my emotions out of sight,

A little bit lonely, and teary eyes.

Everywhere are thorns killing me inside,

Someone hold me, I hope I'll be fine.

SATISH PUTHRAN
SPEAKING SHADOWS
ECHOES FROM THE SILENT CORNERS

All I hallucinate are rainy days,

Those moments which I could never escape.

The hopeful optimist slowly fading in pain,

It asks, Will I ever laugh without breaking away.

© Arjun Malhotra

शापित

कहीं इक कोने में,

दुनिया से परे,

अंधेरे कमरे की जड़ता में

सड़ रही है उसकी साँसें,

खामोशी के नीचे दबा उसका नाम,

वो शापित है।

रूह की कफन में लिपटी,

सपनों के बिखरे कांच पर चलते हुए,

हर घड़ी रेंग रही है हवस की छांव तले,

न चाहत, न राहत,

बस एक परछाई बनकर

तलाश रही है अपने ही वजूद का हिस्सा,

वो शापित है।

अधमरी लाश,

गिद्धों का आखिरी निवाला बनती,

सूरज की बिखरी किरणों से परे,

एक दबी चीख बन

विरान सन्नाटों में खोती जा रही है,

वो शापित है।

© Shruti Bangarwar

BEGINNING

Treading on that sandy shore, awake and afraid,

Gazing into a far land where the stories are made.

As a thought struck me, why again,

In an assumption that it's not an illusion, not again.

Palms dry with the breath of the sun,

And mindful of my meagre stature I trudge on.

I feel the sand draining under my feet in a rush,

As the dissipating waves retreat and again crash.

I feel my legs submerging into the sandy land of the shore,

As I neared the edge more and more.

I feel the heat blind me into a delirious fit,

Blinding me of the visions all but from where my demons await.

Passed the waves and the climb, at last I reach the end,

Toward the scent, deeper and deeper, an endless descent.

And then my head touches the surface,

My body senses the cold and that's where I pause.

On level with the water, my head swivelled to survey

All across fretful and exciteful, to the dream land far away.

I don't know to swim, so like many things I didn't,

To ask where I am going, unlike many times before. I didn't.

Unsure about where to or how, I start swimming,

Deeper and forward with my childish strokes, as each - on its own is just a beginning.

© Rojith. RJ

यह शहर मुझसे बातें करता है

इस शहर की भाग दौड़ में,

इन चमकीली रोशनियों में,

मेरा एक साथी रहता है,

यह शहर मुझसे बातें करता है।

कहता है यह चले जाओ,

जीवन में आगे बढ़ो,

अब मुझसे मोह छुड़ाओ,

मां सी ममता नहीं पीता सा दबा दबा स्नेह करता है,

यह शहर मुझसे बातें करता है।

अपना ना होते हुए भी अपनों सा स्नेह करता है,

मानो मुझे मोहन खुद को नंद बाबा समझता है,

और आज यह मुझे मथुरा छोड़ने को कहता है

यह शहर मुझसे बातें करता है।

छोटे से बड़ा किया इसने,

' याद' शब्द को याद कराया इसने

और आज यह ही मुझे अलविदा कहता है

यह शहर मुझसे बातें करता है।

© वनिशा राय

अजीब कैफ़ियत

एक अजीब कैफ़ियत है, जो तुम्हारी ओर ले जाती है,

तुम मेरी रूह हो, मगर मुझे मुझसे ही जुदा कर जाते हो।

तुम्हें खोना मुश्किल है, पर तुमसे मिलकर भी मैं अधूरी हूँ,

खुद को तलाशने के लिए, शायद तुम्हें भुलाना ज़रूरी है।

© Shruti Bangarwar

जीवनसंगणी

मी अजूनही

तुझीच वाट बघतोय

येशील तु पुन्हा एकदा

जशी भेटलीस सुरुवातीला

अगदी साधी मनमिळाऊ

हट्टही तुझा गोडच होता

प्रत्येक तुझ्या वागण्या-बोलण्यात

घराविषयी गोडवा होता

प्रेम निस्वार्थी असत

हे तूच मला शिकवलं

आपलं कोण परकं कोण

नेहमी मला समजवलं

आज तुझी कमी

प्रत्येक क्षणी जाणवते

आणि उठता बसता मला

तुझीच आठवण येते

खरंच का तू एवढी

माझ्यासाठी सर्व करायची

मला त्रास नको म्हणून

डोळे मिटून शांत निजायची

मी मात्रं तुझ्यासाठी

काहीच करू शकलो नाही

मरूनही तूच जिंकली

जगणे मला जमले नाही

नवरा बायकोच नात

नवरा बायकोच नात

फक्त नात नसतं

नुसतं एकत्र राहणे

तेवढं पुरेस नसत

हात हाती घेतला

तर तेही खुप असत

डोळ्यात डोळे घालून

बोलणं सोपं असत

थकवा दिवसभराचा

एका मिठीत विरून जातो

आणि मनाचा मनातील

रुसवा पुसून जातो

ती कधी त्याच्या

सहज जवळ जाते

आणि हळुवार मनातलं

न सांगता सांगून जाते

तिला त्याच्याशिवाय

करमत थोडंही नाही

आणि त्याचं तिच्याशिवाय

पानही हालत नाही

भांडतात दोघे खूप

तु तु मे मे करतात

आणि पुढच्या क्षणी

दोघे जवळ येतात

नवरा बायकोच नात

खरंच खूपच वेगळं असत

नुसतं एकत्र राहणं

तेवढं पुरेस नसत

© Tata Mahesh Chaudhary

SKY IS THE LIMIT

They say

Sky is the limit

I wonder what it takes to be there

I wonder how it feels to be there

Just like butterflies and birds...

Sky and Clouds, would you ever be mine?

Would you let me know that I am your favourite child!?

Would you mind if I fly!?

You will let me fly, right?

I look at you every evening and Just like your sunset, I want to set free of my worries

Just like how the sun goes down, I want to go down to who I was before,

before all the pains and suffering...

Just like the birds flying

I want to fly, I want to have my own wings...

I wonder what it takes to be there

I wonder how it feels to be there

Those colors scattering at evening are truly colors of my heart

My heart leans for you

My heart hopes for you...

Truly

Sky is the limit...

THE STRENGTH OF MOVING ON

I never thought life would turn out this way. The dreamy world I was living in was nothing more than an illusion. Time changes in the blink of an eye, and the ones we love the most sometimes leave us behind. But the good thing is that time moves on, and we eventually understand that whatever happened was for the best.

I am happy that I taught someone how to live, but the only regret I have is that I forgot to live for myself. Every day was just passing by, filled with my endless tears. Now, I am learning to live where I am, understanding that the past can never return. Every day, I work on improving myself. I no longer have any questions for the person who was never truly mine.

How would he ever understand the pain of betrayal? How would he know what it means to stay committed? I only ever wanted love; I never cared about money or material things. But it's okay—he lost a lot, and I gained even more.

This is life. Even after losing everything, I am learning to live again. I am reconnecting with myself.. I just hope I never remember him again. I loved him deeply, but I will never let this love complete itself. My tears have never stopped, and just like that, my victories will never stop either.

SATISH PUTHRAN
SPEAKING SHADOWS
ECHOES FROM THE SILENT CORNERS

Someone once asked me, "Why are you still holding on to him when you already know everything?" But they wouldn't understand. They never loved, so they will never know—I was never holding on to him.

EMBRACING CHANGE

After a long time, today, I am finally sitting and relaxing. Honestly, I never thought I would change so much or that life would take me this far. Nothing in life is permanent. Now, my only focus is to keep myself happy, no matter what.

If someone wants to talk, they can; if they don't, that's their choice. What truly matters is loving myself, taking care of myself, and always standing up for myself. Earning, staying happy—that's all that really matters.

Today, I don't even think about them anymore, and surprisingly, it feels good. I don't know how, but it just became possible. Everything changes.

Aaj mujhe uski yaad bhi nahi aati, aur ab bahut acha lagne laga hai. Yeh ek jeet hai. Main khud ko evolve hone diya, aur yeh sabse badi baat hai.

RADIATE LOVE, EMBRACE GROWTH

Be happy, love yourself, and embrace the journey of becoming the best version of you.

Nurture your soul, care for your heart, and radiate kindness wherever you go.

Be a light for those in need, a source of love in a world that craves warmth.

Spread love, share joy, and let your presence be a beautiful reminder of compassion and strength.

© Tanzeela Nausheen

FADING MOMENTS : A POEM OF LOST EXPECTATIONS

Some moments slip away not because they are taken from us, but because we watch them fade, helpless. This poem was born from one such moment—an exam that wasn't just a test of knowledge but a test of my self-worth. I had spent the entire year preparing, giving my heart and soul to this one subject, hoping to prove myself. But sometimes, fate has other plans. The paper was easy—too easy—and maybe that's what made it worse. I got lost in my own expectations, trapped in the fear of imperfection, and before I knew it, time had slipped away... just like my dream of a perfect score. This poem carries that loss, that silent regret, and the echo of a moment I couldn't hold onto...

© Tahreem Noor

SLIPPED AWAY

I gave my all, I did my best,

Long nights, no breaks, no time to rest.

But when the moment came to shine,

The clock ran faster than my mind.

The words I knew, they slipped away,

Some dreams take flight, their wings are wide,

Some fall to fate and drift aside.

It's not just sweat, nor battles fought,

But destiny's hand, the things we're taught.

And there they stood, with careless smiles,

Unbothered by the extra miles.

No pages flipped, no notes were made,

Yet all their answers fell in place.

Maybe it's luck, maybe it's fate,

Maybe I learned this all too late,

Some dreams come true,

some never start,

Some break a little piece of heart.

But life moves on, the sun will rise,

For though today was not for me,

Tomorrow holds a mystery.

© Tahreem Noor

BEYOND THE SILENCE

Yet we never collided in this life

Under the different dilemmas

Ghosting around every now and then

Accepting the past that hurts

Never to look upon the scars

Supporting the little steps to walk again

Holding the future dearest to our hearts

In the end, I wish we collide.

© Yuganshi Raj

HAR NAI SUBAH EK NAYA MAUKA ZINDAGI KA

Khone walo ne kho diya muje

Ab paane wale apni kismat par naaz karenge

Kabhi aisa waqt tha jab hum kisi ki khushiyan ya roshni the

Ab kya hua! Mausam hi badal gaya

Waqt har cheez ko badal deta hai.

© Tanzeela Nausheen

HIBISCUS

Rain in Philadelphia is unpredictable. Unlike the monsoon season in Mumbai, it comes and goes as it pleases. I've never been too fond of wet weather—it's all gloom and doom for me. The sky turns slate gray, unnervingly dark even in the daytime, and the mud and murky water drive me nuts.

One such rainy evening, the cold was seeping into my bones, and my heart felt heavy with an unknown sadness. I ducked into a bookstore to escape the chill, only to come face to face with a watercolor painting of a bright red hibiscus flower. Instantly, I was transported back to my childhood in Anand Nagar, Mumbai, India.

Hibiscus flowers, or shoe flowers as we called them, were my grandmother's pride and joy. She loved her hibiscus plants as if they were family. Each morning, she would step outside, her sari draped around her shoulders, and talk to them. Not just a casual "How are you?" but long, drawn-out conversations about the weather, the soil, and the life they shared. She was convinced they understood her.

Sometimes, she would pluck a flower and place it reverently in front of the small statue of Lord Ganesha she worshipped. Hibiscus flowers were his favorite, she always said.

Her hibiscus blooms were a red so vibrant, so alive, they looked like tiny suns scattered across the garden, radiating joy. As a child, I never thought to question her bond with those flowers. Why would I? When I was five and tripped over a rock, scraping my knee raw, she tucked a fresh hibiscus behind my ear and told me its beauty would make the pain vanish. And somehow, it did.

She had to leave her hibiscus shrubs behind when we moved from a cramped one-bedroom apartment to a bigger place. Still, she made it her duty to offer Ganesha a garland whenever she could. When she passed away in January 2004, I placed a single hibiscus flower in front of the statue one last time. I was angry with God for taking her away.

Years passed. I grew older—wiser, maybe—but not wise enough to shake the heaviness that clung to me. A couple of months ago, grief crept up on me again, sharp and unexpected. Even after a decade in Philadelphia, I felt unmoored, as though the city were alien and the world too vast for me to matter in it.

Then something strange started happening.

I began seeing hibiscus flowers everywhere. On my morning walk with my dog, I passed a house I'd never noticed before, its fence dripping with red blossoms. At work, a coworker brought in hibiscus tea. And now, in the bookstore, that painting. It felt uncanny, almost ridiculous. Yet, it was comforting too—like being wrapped in something warm and familiar.

One evening, I came home feeling particularly low. As I unlocked the door, a splash of red caught my eye. A single hibiscus flower bloomed on a plant in the courtyard of my apartment complex. I couldn't remember ever seeing it before. It was as though my grandmother had planted it herself.

I crouched down and touched the velvety petals. For the first time in weeks, I smiled. It wasn't just a flower—it was a whisper from her, a reminder. She had never truly left. Her joy, her love—it lived in those flowers. And it lived in me.

© Mansi Bhagwate

COLLIDING HEARTS

Before you I didn't know myself

Lost in the world that didn't exist

I tried to perfect myself

Gone were those days after i met you,

It was for sure that our hearts were meant to collide

After we fell in the dark abyss

Deep down we went

Only to see the light in the end

Then i knew we were meant to emerge stronger ever after

© Simran Sahoo

THOUGHTS

- जिंदगी हैरान कर देती है

वक्त बेतलब देती है तू
कर न सके कभी वक़्त पर काम
तो नया एहसास से रुबरु करा देती है तू।

- इन डगमग सी राहों में

हम को न परखना
हम तो ठहरे रोज़ के राही, मुसाफ़िर न समझना।

- सपने पूरे होतें हैं

बिना ज़नून के नहीं
एक बार ज़नून को आज़ माओ तो सही
सपने कम हो जाऐंगे।

© Supriya Sharma

LOVE : A QUESTION WITHOUT ANSWERS

What is love? Is your relationship with your ex called love? How do you know its love? How do you define love? Damn! We used to call ourselves true lovers but at the end it's just a broken relation. Isn't love supposed to be unbreakable or is it breakable? How can one find that they are in love? How can one know that they are in love with someone? Is love blind? Or is it any illusion we create to blind ourselves? Does love hurt? If it hurts then why search for it? Isn't love supposed to heal a person? Does love find us or we find love? Is love simple or is it complicated as it seems? Does love exists? If love exists then it should have a meaning right? If love doesn't exist why do we thrive to find it throughout our lives? Is love worth finding or it isn't? These many questions arise from a single feeling or word or an illusion we put ourselves in. what are the answers for it then? Don't know right! Some people think that love is everything and some say it isn't. Which is correct? either or neither? We still don't know. No matter how hard you try, you cannot explain love. Why because it's like infinity in mathematics, no matter which number you choose there is always another one in infinity. Let me rephrase that for you. If you think love has meaning or it doesn't. It's upto you to decide that. You can even say that love is similar to paradox. That means you can't prove either yourself or others. It's a contradiction no one has yet defined exactly but we find our own versions of contradiction about love and live with it. If you ever want to find what love is, then do it in your own way and embrace it with all your heart. ♡

© Sai Mallareddy

MY INNER THOUGHTS

Ah, I have many thoughts in my mind,

Nowhere is safe to open up the heart;

My soul doth work on a path to find,

Hark, the essence of life is noble art;

O, people hath golden jewels to live,

'Tis never be the right thing to follow;

Love's always immaculate to give

For people who are above and below.

Whatever I gift with my humbleness,

People get rid of it for their merriment;

They degrade my magnanimousness

By making sarcasms on establishment.

My inner thoughts nurture me strong

When people expect me to do wrong

PODCAST WITH MR. MIND

Hi there..., Mr. Mind!!! How are you?

Oh dear! Hi Buddy, after all these years, you finally realized my importance. It's good that you care about me.

Care? I need to confront Mr. Mind and yes, I never asked, maybe I wasn't aware, maybe I never felt your existence nor tried to see beyond your blabber. I always felt its me ... until I realized it's not me, it's you!!

Ohh...hold on buddy, glad that you know that I was always with you, but what do you wish to know about? Your heartbreak? Your pain? Your embarrassment? Your failures? Your loss?

Hahahha, as expected, is there anything new to offer Mr

Mind? You always know my menu and you serve the same dishes with additional “TADKA” every time.

Yes buddy, you like it when you are served like this. You enjoy when I fry your future plans with frustrations, you like it when I chop your happiness and serve with some seasonings of sadness. You enjoy when I roast your reality and push you into your past regrets. You have been consuming them throughout your life and I just followed my routine now.

Ohh, is it, you think it’s a joke? I like them? Seriously? Why did you serve me rejection when all I wanted is to love? Why did you leave me with rage and anger, when all I wanted was some answers to cure my soul? Why didn’t you stop me when I chose penny over passion? Why do you push me into the infinite loop of sadness and leave me with bundles of unanswered mysteries to solve? I wasn’t enjoying it even a single bit.

Wasn’t all these your choice? You allowed the agony of rejection to rejoice in you. You had a choice to reform, you chose to remorse. Your 1000 “pleases” were plunged into pothole. You had a choice to put a full stop, but you pleased 1001th time. You had the choice to pursue your passion, instead you procrastinated. You never questioned what I offered. You never resisted, you always filled these in your memories and these were your comfort meal.

Shall I ask you something? Why didn't you tell me all this before? My life would have been so much better.

Ahh, not again, I probably did. Many a times.. but you were so busy justifying yourself, to yourself again and again under the guidance of your guru Prof. Heart. Its my job to test , track and trick with thousands of thoughts , but choosing the one you want, directing them to the destiny you decide and finally the way you want to feel is ultimately your “CHOICE”.

Ufff.. Why are you so complicated? Why can’t you just be smooth and simple? Why is it so hard to understand you?

Buddies, my conversations with you are purely based on what you allow yourself to consume and feed. You may feed it from your surroundings, parents or your past." I am you. What you think and I become". So sorry to extract all these quotes from your 10th text book, but that's the truth. Okay! Fine... I want my menu to be changed. Help me out to customize. Can you?

Oh sure, as i already said. “It’s your choice”. You can also have a menu filled with latte of love, juices of joy and happiness with an extra pinch of positivity with slice of self confidence. You can also avail the special offers to anesthetize your anxiety with mindset of abundance and meditations. Finally you can always taste the dessert of reaching your destiny. Would you like it buddy?

Yes! Why not? I am ready to dive into this, if you also want to............then...

HAVE A PODCAST WITH YOUR MR.MIND.

© Akshay R Rao

जाऊ दे

कधी ऐकला आहे का स्वतःच्या आतला आवाज?

मी ऐकला आहे. जेव्हा डोळे मिटून स्वतःला अनुभवायला लागतो ना तेव्हां वेगळीच मजा येते.

जगाच्या व्यवहारातून आपल्या आत शिरताना लाखो विचारांचा गोंधळ असतो, पण त्या गोंधळातुन निसटन्यास एक एकच शब्द मदत करतो, तो म्हणजे 'जाऊ दे'.

या शब्दाची वेगळीच मजा आहे, आपण सर्व काही विसरून जायला लागतो आणि हृदयाचा आवाज आपल्याला आकर्षित करून घेतो. जेव्हा स्वतःच्या हृदयाचा आवाज आपण ऐकतो तेव्हा अनुभवायला मिळते ती एक विलक्षणीय शांतता.

ही शांतता आपल्याला स्वतःची ओळख करून देते व आपल्या मनातील सर्व शंकाना स्थगित करते आणि आपल्या समोरील प्रश्नांसाठी एक नवीन मार्ग काढण्यासाठी मदत करते. 😊

जो कोणी हा लेख वाचत असेल ना त्यांनी हा अनुभव नक्कीच घ्या. हा लेख आतल्या विचारांचा आहे, जाऊ दे येवढ जर म्हणाता आलं ना तर आनंदाने जगन खूप सोपं होतं.

© मयु कदम

DESTINY OF HER OWN MAKING

History never forgives the black sheep,

A woman who clad in mischief,

But this untamed creature, as they say

Do not care

For she sways in the swing of an epoch

From one moment to another,

Never looking back at the voluptuous uproar and mayhem with a desire to engulf her.

She walks through the rumbles of her mother, grandmother, great grandmother, and through every woman who on the instructions of men tries to bind her,

In the chains of grace, duty, sensitivity, forgiveness –

But she molds a key for every lock ever made

Her ferocity to take the next stride and run through the aches of time,

Chasing the sun, widening the galore of her wings,

Like the flower that gets trampled by the feet of many,

yet survives to grow

By making way through the cracks in laden path

History never forgives the black sheep,

But who cares about the archives written and traded by men for centuries,

It's the spiel of men who claimed victory on the heap of bodies that exhibited gallantry, telling of men who were ruthless through every bend and end,

Telling of men who thought that a lady is an object of adoration like a golden bird, Glorious, but only when held captive not the confessions of a woman,

For she needs no narrative to stamp her existence in the expanse of cosmos,

She is an equal part of everything

From smallest quark to the mightiest star

Even in the dust of the dead, she exists equally;

Immortality is not her rave,

Destiny of actions is what she chases.

MAKING ENDS MEET

She loving looked at the face of her little new born. When she heard the doctor come in and stand beside her, she asked her, in a voice tired from yet another child-birth and patient from the many years of raising children.

"I hope you've done what I asked you to...."

Before she could answer her entire life flashed in front of her: she was only 18 and he was 19. It was love in the times of unemployment and living off the little that their parents earned from their hours of toiling away in the high-rises of the city and returning to the slimy slums at night. After losing their land to greedy money lenders in the village both their parents had come to the city to make ends meet.

Truly, madly, deeply in love these lovers spent their whirlwind courtship period by regularly stealing money from their parents. It was the simplest way for them to make ends meet.

When the parents found out, not only about the stealing but about the relationship they were furious. "He is an unemployed youth; will he be able to feed you? I have been toiling hard to raise you and pay for your brother's schooling and you go about spending all the money on that good for nothing boy!" screamed her father.

The couple took a cue from the steps the hero-heroine in a Bollywood blockbuster who were also madly in love had taken, they eloped! They were all starry eyed about how she would set up the new house, cook and clean, wait for him at the door to return from work.

The stage was set but the script took a wild twist. To begin with they had to settle for a small hut in a slum in the suburbs of Mumbai far away from their parents home, to stay away from getting caught and having to return home. The first few months they lived off the money some friends and well-wishers had given as a wedding gift. He still hadn't found any employment. The money was dwindling. The debt at the grocery stores were rising. Little did she know that his debt at gambling at the local country bar and liquor bills were rising too. In all this mess, she also got pregnant. Once he got to know about the child, he started drinking out of anxiety of how he would make ends meet and beating her under the influence of alcohol.

She didn't know what to do, whom to turn to... Thanks to the wafer thin walls of the hut, the neighbour lady had heard her entire ordeal. She got her a job as a dishwasher at an apartment nearby. That's how she started earning, it was seven years since that day and she was a mother of four lovely little girls, growing up in the same small little hut that she had now made home. Her husband was still unemployed and a drunkard, she still loved him dearly.

"Yes, we tied the tubes..." said the doctor.

She smiled contented knowing now that the doctor has made the ends of the tubes meet, she could finally work make ends meet, cause there would be no more extra mouths to feed and she had given birth to a son who would someday in this patriarchal society, take care of the family and of her.

© Preeti Gujar

LIFE

!!!!!!!!! Life is unpredictable !!!!!!

For someone it's the bed of roses....

For someone it's thorns of life ...

For someone it's just a game ...

For someone it's only for fame...

Life is so unpredictable..

There will be a time where you feel like a hell....

There will be a time where your solitude will be your best friend....

There will be a time where you have to

Wipe up your tears by yourself....

There will be a time where a smile is just to hide your pain.....

Life is so unpredictable..

Where you will meet someone Who will be your love one....

Where you can be trust one who can give Your heart one....

Where you can one and can say this is mine one....

Life is so unpredictable.. it is unpredictable......

MOON

It's 3 in the night

I blow my insecurities like I blow a cig

Looking at the stars I wonder what does it hold?

Does life also come with beautiful darkness?

My versions talk to me loudly

They make me deaf

I say life is beautiful but I reply it is hell

I'm supposed to live,

Things will be fine

I guess...

Nah!

I'm supposed to leave myself behind

And fly

I want to touch that sky and dance

Oh, it's the moon again

Trying to make me smile

And there, the pole star showing me the right direction

But is it right?

I lit another cig

And now life is lil more dark

It's not black spots on white sheet

It's white spots on black sheet

With cold wind came some cold emotions

Nothing makes me cry anymore

You leave me I die, I die in peace

Death is my comfort now I talk to death I'm having my time

I'm strong in this moment

Or vulnerable I suppose

But isn't being vulnerable a strength in itself?

I go to sleep

With smile on my lips

In my mind I cry, I take myself in my arms

And

I love myself for hating myself

Is this my life or is it me

Who is wrong

I think our bond is

I know my bond with death would make me feel alive the most

Oh it's 5 now

With sun my hopes rise too

A new morning and a new start

I didn't sleep all night

I would sleep tomorrow

I'm coming back to reality

Leaving all my illusions behind

No death isn't my companion, my life is

And my people are

With deep breaths I inhale some hopes

I'm standing now

My knees hurt but I'm strong

And I'm living

Hope is like water to life

Living without it, is putting a hold on death

I hope and I live

This is me and my life

I can create it and I will

With moon my insecurities go down too

They may come up tomorrow,

I'm not letting the tomorrow come.

© Shruti Bangarwar

MORTAL REALM

Flowers don't bloom all eternity

Rain doesn't always fall

Sunshine is short-lived

Moon can only brighten so much.

Names rolling off my tongue-

Like a flickering candle

One day, must extinguish.

The stars adorning the night sky

Must one day disappear.

Soulless, the world is

Transient, never immortal.

Sure, there is age

Never permanence

Even words that ebb to flow

Fade into the pages of history.

Conflicted with thoughts

I hear you say my name

A weight lifted off my mind.

Rest assured,

I am here,

For sometime I will be here

It matters not how it was before me

Nor how it will be after

With the wind brushing my hair

The sun kissing my cheeks

Laughter filling my ears

I am content with mortality.

© Killada Shreevani

ECHOES OF THE OCEAN

Secrets in the streams

Distill into the ocean dreams

Sea salt, our treasured memories

Stars trip over moonlight

Just to hear those dreams breathe

Falling stars, crossed oceans

Released from your storm

Suddenly, the vagrancy

Of the moon is home

You are a nightmare

Dressed like a daydream

Silently, oceans roar, breaking up

I was still alive

When you dropped me

From forever

You hit,

Like the sky,the earth,and the sea

Every part of me

I swallowed

Ash - My phoenix flew

Unfeathered

Dripping from the sea

A universe lost in waxing light

I'm resurrected every night

SATISH PUTHRAN
SPEAKING SHADOWS
ECHOES FROM THE SILENT CORNERS

It hurt, then hurt more

To unlearn everything,

Then learn more

Now that's everythings over

What can I do

Pretend nothing happen

Who hums with us

The dull chorus

Of lonliness?

© Magie Gadidesi

LIFE IS A DILEMMA

The more you sit idle, the more worthless you feel

The faster you wish to recover, the slower you heal

Fed up of all the time getting a raw deal

Broken parts of yourself are what you're trying to conceal

You seem bombarded with all the emotional and gloomy sensations

Unable to recall the positive affirmations

Sadly, life is full of terms and conditions

And now you're a crybaby in everybody's perceptions

That one heavy sack of burden you carry

Making your shoulders always feel sore

Questioning 'Why me?' to the universe every time

Not wanting to ask for help from anybody anymore

Don't you drown yourself into the pool of sadness

Instead push yourself to learn to swim in the ocean of madness

Come out of the penumbra of darkness

Step into the world of brightness

Cause you're born to win no matter if you're still clueless

Lost all hope? Self-trust is the need of the hour

You always have be aware of your self power

When tough times come, do not withdraw; just be strong

Enjoy all the happy moments cause they won't last long

Make your own rules, break them

People are anyway gonna question your morality

Stop living in this cosmos of duality

Come out of your cocoon and face the reality

© Deepa Vasant Shenoy

BLACK ROSE

The dewy petals be voluptuous the many as any blooming buds,

The subtle shades as well do sing of the lightning and rain in the distant clouds.

Elated do the wind and the weeds drift close to the musky fragrance,

Along come the watchers crawling and flying, as infectious as to any a magical performance.

Then Pray tell thee, the untold darkness, the dusky luminescence,

Why do the dripping rain drops and the slumping leaves weep of thy desolate loneliness. Does not the fireflies crowd around thee like so many dazzled suitors, For I see the bewitched admirers thy kin so easily allures? Does not the merry day embellish thy hue to a more rapturousk?

Pray, where be thy luminant gleam in the nightly gloom turning thine visage picturesque?

Do not the folks and the infants lose their selves in boundless euphoric glee

Witnessing the iridescence of inky blackness thine, or in uncertain fear did they flee?

Is it a beatific irony that the majestic creation thou might be,

Or a mysterious trial for the insatiable mankind that be?

For the shaded beauty or the barbed stem, the gleaming tar or the flavorsome poison you call it be,

The eternal perjury, the uncertainty thy wild hubris blossom be.(ye is hoga shayad not sure just aise hi caught my eye edit krte wakt dekh lena)

© Rojith. RJ

KHAMOSH HU MAIN

Khamosh hu mai...!!

Ek alag sa shor hai man me,

Jese koi bhuchal chal raha ho jeevan me,

Magar, shabdo se jese naata tut chuka ho mera,

Kuch is tarah khamosh hu mai.

Kehne ko sekdo baatein hai,

Magar bharosa ab kisi par bhi nahi hai,

Kis se baatu ye sawal har pal hai,

Magar, bharosa karne se pal pal darta ab mera man hai.

Ghav itne gehre hai,

Ki man, mastisk dono hi ab thak gae hai,

Bas ye jeevan maano bojh hai,

Kyuki intezaar ab aakhri saans ka hai.

Apmaan itne sahe hai,

Ki har seema paar ho chuki hai,

Ab apno se b koi vaasta bacha nahi hai,

Kyuki ghaav inhi ke sabse jyada hai.

Nahi ab kisi se ummeed hai,

Nahi ab kisi ka intezaar hai,

Jeevan ki is dohare safar me,

Bas Maut ka yun intezaar hai.

Kuch tarah se ab ruth chuki hu mai,

Koi laakh mana le par ab maan na paungi mai,

Sikhayatein to lab par hazaar hai,

Magar ab Sirf Khamosh hu mai.

Sirf Khamosh hu mai.....!!!

© Deep Thinker

यादों की लिपि

तुम्हारी याद में...

मैं तुम्हें कागज़ पर पिरोना चाहता हुँ

मेरी कॉफी सुख चुकी है

उससे लिखना चाहता हूं तुम्हारे रेश्मी होठों को

और रंगना चाहता हूं वही नील

जो सूखने पर सुर्ख लाल हो जाएंगी

बिल्कुल हमारे इश्क़ की तरह।

मैं कोई रंगरेज़ या कलाकार नहीं हूं।

न ही मुझे हुनर है आँखों को तराशने का।

मगर पढ़ना सीखा है मैने, आंखों को,

आसमानों को और उड़ते परिंदों को।

तुम सबकी भाषा एक ही लेख की है

आज़ादी की लिपी!

SATISH PUTHRAN
SPEAKING SHADOWS
ECHOES FROM THE SILENT CORNERS

तुम्हारी मरासिम आंखों में लहजा है

नज़ाकत जैसे इजाज़त मांगती हो

उनमें नज़रबंद होकर रहने का।

उनमे ठिकाने हैं थकावट के मरहम के।

जिनको देखते ही ख़्वाब जाग उठते

और मुझसे पूछते हैं।

ये पहचाने हैं या अजनबी।

मैं अचम्बा सा रहता हूँ

तुम्हें घूरने और अच्छे से घूरने में

शिद्दत भी है और सुकून भी।

मैं उसी में व्यस्त हुँ।

मुझे इन सवालों का कोई ख़बर नहीं।

ज़्यादा ज़रुरी लगे तो मुझे घूर लेना

तुम पा जाओगी सारे उत्तर

मेरी आँखों में।

©® रजत कुमार दलाई

ECHOES OF HURT

That's the thing about anger,

It substitute hurt.🔄

Hurt you don't know how to deal with,

Hurt you didn't even knew existed

within the grasp of your soul.☄🌠

At times, I get too scared;

too scared to leave people around me,

too scared to let go of things that surrounds me.

See that's the thing, I'm not good with changes. 🎭

The idea of sharing an underrated song

burns my soul bcoz people ruin beautiful things.😑

And the world is running out of those.

I have never been so busy to keep the world out that

I forget,

I locked myself in. 🔒

© Rahul Jhawar

INNER CRY

Leave a spot in your heart intact

A secret room you can always run to

When things get dark,

Fill it with what touches your soul the most,

The tiny things that lead you back to your real self,

Conversations with God, music, books, memories, even your favorite sip of coffee, run with all your heart to

whatever no chaos can ever break it,

Break slowly that special air of your own world,

Where you really belong,

Revive those sacred even illogical dreams,

But this is you, this where your strength resides,

Where you recharge all your tired senses,

This is why you don't surrender...

© Ashrin Mathew

संघर्ष: स्वतःशी आणि परिस्थितीशी

मानसिक संघर्षातून मार्ग काढून जिवन आनंदाने कसं जगावं...!!!!

मानवी जीवन म्हटलं की इच्छा ,आकांक्षा असणारच आणि त्या पूर्ण करण्यासाठी मग संघर्षही करावाच लागतो...कधी परिस्थितीशी , व्यक्तींशी तर कधी स्व:ताशी सुद्धा...!!

संघर्ष जेव्हा परिस्थितीमुळे असतो तेव्हा आपल्या जवळच्या व्यक्तींशी मनमोकळा संवाद साधणं त्यांचा सल्ला/मदत घेणं हा संघर्षातून मार्ग काढण्याचा सोप्पा मार्ग आहे. मात्र त्यासाठी तसे संबंध / मित्रमंडळी जाणीवपूर्वक तयार करावे लागतात ,जपावे लागतात. तर कधी त्या- त्या विषयातील तज्ज्ञांचां सल्ला घेऊन संघर्षातून मार्ग काढण्याचा प्रयत्न करावा लागतो. (उदा. गंभीर आजारामुळे तणाव निर्माण झाल्यास डॉक्टरांचा सल्ला घेणं व त्याप्रमाणे उपचार घेणं)

एखाद्या व्यक्तीमुळे /मतभेदांमुळे संघर्ष सदृष्य परिस्थिती निर्माण झाल्यास संयमाने , संवाद साधणं, आपली बाजू मांडणं आणि त्या व्यक्तीची बाजू समजून घेणे आवश्यक

असतं. आणि त्यातून काही बाबतीत तडजोडीचं धोरण ठेवून तर काही बाबींकडे सरळ दुर्लक्ष करून संघर्ष टाळता येऊ शकतो.

पण जेव्हा संघर्ष स्व:ताशीच असतो तेव्हा जवळच्या व्यक्तींना , विश्वासात घेऊन आडपडदा न ठेवता संवाद साधणं आवश्यक ठरतं. आणि त्यांनी दिलेला परखड सल्ला समजून घ्यावा. पण घेतलेला निर्णय , त्याची अंमलबजावणी व त्याचे परिणाम ह्याचा विचार करून तारतम्य बाळगून मार्ग काढावा... म्हणजे "ऐकावे जनांचे-करावे मनाचे" प्रमाणे...!!

दैनंदिन जिवनात जेव्हा लहान - सहान चूका (जसं की दूध उतू गेलं...इत्यादी)आपल्या कडून झाल्या मुळे मानसिक आंदोलनं होतात ....हाही एक संघर्षाचाच प्रकार

त्यावेळास पन्नास- शंभर कामं केली तर एक - दोन चूका होणारच , अशी स्व:ताची समजूत काढून स्व:ताला माफ करावं.

काही वेळेस, संघर्षाचं कारण-मुद्दा तपासून घ्यावा. एखाद्या

तकलादू कारणासाठी संघर्ष करून आपण आपला वेळ -शक्ती वाया तर घालवत नाही ना? हे जरूर तपासून घ्यावे.

असे संघर्ष टाळावेत.

आणि काहीही झालं... कितीही टोकाचा संघर्ष निर्माण झाला तरी....ही एक तात्पुरती परिस्थिती (passing phase) असून मी ह्यातून संयमाने , चिकाटीने , जिद्दीने ,इतरांच्या मदतीने व परमेश्वरावर विश्वास ठेवून मार्ग काढणारचं ,असा सकारात्मक दृष्टिकोन ठेवावा.

© सौ. मुग्धा राणे

शक्ति स्वरूपा

प्रारंभ तू , अंत तू,

ब्रह्माची निर्मिती तू....

भाव तू , भक्ती तू,

आदिशक्ती नारी तू....

प्रेम तू , त्याग तू,

स्वतःची सखी तू....

सत्य तू , अस्तित्व तू,

जगण्याची नवी उमेद तू....

मोह तू , माया तू,

परीसासम स्पर्श तू....

मुक्त तू , स्वछंदी तू,

गुणगुणावे असे गीत तू....

जीत तू , यशस्वी तू,

विजयी ललकार तू....

निडर तू , निर्भय तू,

पाण्यापरी निर्मळ तू....

गत तू , वर्तमान तू,

सोनेरी भविष्य तू....

© सौ.विजया श्री थोरवे

DAUGHTER'S LIFE

I never bother about the bloody systems of caste, religion, region or any discriminations that challenge the human dignity, respect and decorum", thundered the leader of the innocent masses, known for his oratory skills of high standard. The audience felt that they should also shed these masks to be ideal citizens.

At home his daughter hesitatingly introduced him her lover who belonged to the different caste, religion, region and a poor illiterate family. The father became speechless. In his rage, he ordered his henchmen to carry out the honour killing. The daughter and others do not know his masked face.

© Rangeesh Chandrasekar

BEHIND THE SMILE

The mask of a smile on her face everyone can see,

But behind that mask, there's a different she,

when I notice and asked if she is fine? she again smiles and flies like a bee,

She smiles and fasts just for her husband, and son coz she finds herself happy as a devotee,

We the men never understand and think that it's her duty but think once what's our duty towards that she?.

When we say it's gonna be okay, but there's no sunshine ray,

Does anyone try to know what's going inside her?

Does anyone try to hear her silent cry?

Does anyone try to hear her screaming?

Say now

Anyone?

anyone?

anyone?

AM I ALONE?

I think to cut all connections,
I think I am alone.
Afraid that my ideals were a dream,
Have nothing left to postpone.

I gave my all,
And got nothing back.
I saw the reality in front of my eyes,
I didn't even ask for that.

Was it all fake,
The heart I poured out,
The friends at stake,
All went down the drain.

Made me a realist from an idealist,

Made me believe people go away.

They were selfish in the small moments,

And then called me best one to date.

This fakeness you can't decide,

Are the relationships just a vicious play,

Or is something left inside.

© Arjun Malhotra

SHE WAS ME!

From up above I saw a tree the size of a beetle,

As I shrouded in the cloud's mantle.

I cleaved to the moon,

I felt safe like I was in my cocoon,

I ate chips made of the already set-sun,

And the cloud shaped like a bun.

Made of lightning was my throne,

My chariot was made of stars that shone,

The cool breeze made me feel free,

As I forgot the world below me,

I no longer breathed death in every breath,

I was liberated of all my inhibitions, I understood me in all my depth.

My soul beseeched the Creator, where were you amidst my cries?

SATISH PUTHRAN
SPEAKING SHADOWS
ECHOES FROM THE SILENT CORNERS

Where were you in my grief, my agony, my sighs?

I beheld the dark skies,

I sought again and again and got no replies,

I was encumbered with the weight of the lies;

That had been fed into me, all the stories and the smiles,

About the Creator, about life, about living.

And then a broken star fell from the sky still burning,

Spiralling across the dark, its trail began writing,

"It was a play, a game, a stage,

Where you could be anything, my dame,

Why did you wish to be like the others, the same?

You are glorious, you are different,

You are magnificent and brilliant,

Why did you try to fit into the moulds and the rules?

That were set by tyrants and fools,

You were sent to heal the wounded souls,

Why did you hurt the ones who loved you the most?

With words shaped like a dagger, why did you duel?

And why did you wound yourself with thoughts so cruel,

Why did that golden heart that loved without measure,

Break itself into pieces every day asunder."

My eyes were opened, finally my Creator I did see;

My Saviour in a reflection in the Sea,

All along SHE WAS ME.

And suddenly I felt like I won over everything or that I didn't need to be anything,

Because I was already loved,

Already valued, a special part of the cosmos,

I was made of Stardust, broken diamonds and primrose.

There was no pressure of outdoing or succeeding,

I was void of the fear of failure, because up there it was not about achieving or competing,

It was about Healing, Feeling and Loving.

I sat there rejoicing with nature beloved;

As I knew, up there, I was being loved.

As the breeze flashed through my skin,

I felt everyone, up there, were my kin.

As I sat there rejoicing with nature beloved;

I knew, up there, I was being loved.

I felt at peace, after so many years,

When my mother's voice rang in my ears,

'Wake up or you'll be late for school.'

But this time I woke up not as the fool,

But completely calm and cool,

For I was touched by the Creator in my dream,

And she resides in me, and I am she, no matter how hard the world may seem.

© Rachel Raju Alice

AFTER A TORRENT

Do you people think,

That we think, bizarre?

No! We think bright,

But you're the one in the night.

When we show our colours,

Then you show your buck.

We don't wanna be pink and blue,

To be stuck in the stinking glue.

We're as vivid as a rainbow,

But y'all are as ruinous as a rain cloud.

Why, being so sad for us?

For us, being what we really are.

We don't have to be,

Or can't be fixed;

'Cause we're not broken.

We're just born this way.

© Joel

WAVES OF SELF-DISCOVERY

Everything was ok until that day.

Suddenly a silent wave took my breath away.

Everything felt different for me the next day.

Other than one thing that always made me unique,

It's an absence that many people feel today.

And now I'm with the waves,

Waiting for one more moment to reach the shore again.

So that I can watch my loved ones missing my presence.

I can now rejoice of realising my worth

The worth which I have never felt before.

Darker night and unstoppable feelings.

I've always felt haunted and then realised a truth,

noone can help me rather than myself.

As a human my emotions are limitless.

SATISH PUTHRAN
SPEAKING SHADOWS
ECHOES FROM THE SILENT CORNERS

I'm subjected to a lots of questions.
And I found that it's my responsiblity to get answers
For everything that my heart seeks.

Yes I felt I was mad.
But it doesn't made me feel bad.
My thoughts were always intern,
They hesitated to subsist.
Many forced me to pretence,
But I refused to survive being caged.
Thoughts always surged into my heart,
Keeping me awake even in the dark.
Let me wander and retrieve in my dreams,
From where I lost my thoughts,
And started my journey of hope.

खामोशी की बातें

रात के खामोशी में भी

तुम्हारे बातें मुझे सुखून दिलाता है

इन्ही बातों से सही

तुमने मुझे अंधेरे से भी

मुहब्बत करना सिखाया ।

© Abirami Aji

इंतज़ार की खामोशियाँ

झरोके पर बैठकर... पुराने गीतों को सुनकर

मन कुछ बहक गया है...

आज शाम ज्यादा अपनी सी लगती है

मानो मेरी बातें बिना कहे समझ रही है...

ख्यालों में कोई है...

एहसास है...

उसका ख्वाब है

बस झलक नहीं दिखती....

चेहरे पर मुस्कान है उसके इंतज़ार की....

इंतज़ार फिर ऐसी ही शाम की...

पर इस बार एहसास नही, मौजूदगी की..!!

© अंशिता राय

RISING UNBROKEN : ALWAYS HEALING

Do I really need the person who hurt me

To come and say, "Yes, I hurt you,"

And ask for forgiveness?

Yes, it would be good to hear,

But do I really need it?

Do I not already know how deep the pain was

When I felt it in every part of me?

Do I need him to tell me how much it hurt?

Do I need his permission to heal—

Something I don't need, yet still, a part of me wants?

Because I believed my relief would come

When he acknowledged the pain he put me through,

And maybe that's true...

But the real truth is—

The one who caused my pain cannot take it away.

I have to heal myself.

I cannot expect the one who broke me

To gather my broken pieces

And put me back together.

That is not his right.

Someone who had the power to destroy me,

And chose to use that power—

Why would I trust them to rebuild me?

Do I really need the person who hurt me

To be the one to heal me?

EK AFSANA

Mohabbat mein bheekh mangna suna hoga na,

Uske sath chalne ki koshish mein kabhi khud ko bhool baitha tha,

Dhyan hi nahi diya ke agar kabhi wapas akele lautna pada,

To kaise lautenge, kaise sambhalenge?

Jiske piche mohabbat ke naam per bhagate chale gaye

Usi ne tumhein dhakka diya tho,

kaise sambhalenge?

Ek tarfa mohabbat toh nahin thi ye

kyunki dil todne ke liye hi sahi

Dil toh usne bhi lagaya tha apne

Peeche bas bhagane ke liye hain, pyar tho usne bhi jataya tha

Jise waqt nahin tumhare haal janne ka tumhein behaal karne ke liye hi sahi waqt tho usne bhi lagaya tha

Aur mohabbat ki bheekh mang rahi thi main par bhool gayi thi jis mohabbat ke liye tadapte hain log woh mohabbat beshumar usse jaise per kabhi maine uspar lutaya tha.

Aise log se mohabbat nahi aati, aise log per taras aata hai

© Tanzeela Nausheen

THE LUXURY OF LETTING GO

There was a time when Aisha used to chase people—friends who forgot to reply, family who took her presence for granted, and even strangers who barely noticed her efforts. She believed that holding on was a sign of strength, but with time, she realized that letting people lose her was a different kind of self-respect.

One evening, she sat on her rooftop, phone face down, untouched for hours. The world had made mobile phones the new luxury, but for her, the real luxury was peace—watching the moon instead of notifications, embracing solitude instead of shallow conversations.

As she gazed at the sky, she thought about those who had drifted away. Some left out of neglect, some because they didn't value her. But she had stopped mourning losses. "Khone walo kho diye," she whispered to herself, "ap paane wale apni kismat par naaz krenge."

She smiled, knowing that the ones who truly mattered would find their way to her—not through texts, but through time, effort, and presence. And that was enough.

EMBRACE THE NOW : OVERCOMING FEAR & TAKING THE LEAP

The truth is, you'll never feel fully ready.

Take that leap of faith.

Stop trying to wait for the "perfect" moment because it doesn't exist.

Your moment is now.

Your potential is endless.

Don't let fear stand in your way of a new chapter.

© Tanzeela Nausheen

THE BRAVERY IN GOODBYE

TANZEELA NAUSHEEN & LATE. SUPRIYA

I lost my friend to CANCER.

"She [SUPRIYA] was full of life and truly curious. She would ask a million questions not out of politeness or for small talk but because she was genuinely interested in people and cared for their stories. She would tell me, if you want to help someone in their time of need, don't ask what you can do for them, just be there and do it. I couldn't have asked for a better friend. She's missed beyond measure."

"Cancer was a taboo, and when it hit someone close to u, we didn't know which way to turn and suggest something. I was lost and so confused. Some people around them, who were equally ignorant, made them feel like it was the end of the world. It was a very harrowing and testing period for them"

"Supriya was such a brave and happy girl".

"While the family was worried about Supriya, she always reassured them that treatment and getting better were way easier things to tackle, since the diagnosis was in. She never once felt otherwise. "She was such a brave girl,"

"For 4 year, from October 2018 to July 2022, Supriya's family tried getting her better. On 12 July 2022, she succumbed to the disease and lost the battle. "The loss is something that I just cannot describe. I met her once in October 2021."

"It pushed me into a very dark hole"

"Specially for her family it's feeling like a stone. The family oscillated between anger and sadness."

“It might take sometime for her family, Specialy (mom and brother) to come out of the shock. Now it's our time to support emotionally for patients and caregivers. Support as much as possible [ZINDAGI BADI HONI CHAHIYE LAMBI NAHI]”

"This is my way of carrying Supriya's name forward. Death cannot be the end of her story."

© Tanzeela Nausheen

- Readers this is a real, heart touching & heart breaking story of loosing a true friend.

♡ INTEZAAR NHI...... MOHABBAT HAIN ♡

Intezaar hai...

Intezaar hai lafzon ka..

Intezaar hai kuch ehsaas ka..

Intezaar sikha deta hai..

Intezaar har cheez ka jawab de jata hai...

Zindagi me kuch shuru karna bahut mushkil hota hai,

Jab shuru kar do toh bahut asaan ho jata hai..

Dil hamesha bechain hota hai..

Kaamyabi ki aur chalne lagta hai.

Khud ko pehchane se zaroori,

Khud ko uss kabil banane ke liye tawajjuh dena zaroori hai.

Apne aap se roobaru hone ke liye,

Har din khud se taluq rakhna zaroori hai,

Warna yeh waqt kab guzar jaye..

Mohabbat muqtazar nahi,

Zindagi bhar hoti hai.

Mohabbat khud chalkar aati hai,

Uski talaash nahi karte.

Mohabbat khushiyan le aati hai.

Mohabbat dil ka sukoon de jati hai.

♡ INTEZAAR NHI......MOHABBAT HAIN ♡

HEALING THROUGH THE COLORS

another piece is missing a gash in the flesh.

blood oozes, black and bold and I must mend.

green radiates

brown steadies

ivory sparkles

ripples and rhythm

and I become whole again.

© Mansi Bhagwate

THE INHERITANCE OF SCARS

I wasn't born with chains,

But i was taught to wear them.

I wasn't her blood and bones,

I hated her at first-

For stealing my dear dad,

But that was before,

I knew the monster in him,

Who came alive,

The magic potion wasnt alcohol,

Or substances,

But the glorified male ego.

I saw the bruises and battles,

Fights Over silly little things.

Red eyes and tears,

Yet she stood strong,

swallowing her fears.

For you,she said often,

I'll stay still for long.

This was a monthly ritual,

As certain as rising of moon,

As inevitable as blood and pain,

Menses and discharge,

So feminine and divine.

The stories were always the same-

She had to compromise,

She had to endure.

She had to make it work-

To leave would be a shame.

She has to submit,

She has to cry-silently,

But in vain.

The last to eat,

Scraping the leftovers on the plate-

But it wasnt about the role,

For it was always cherished.

By her,not them,

but the worth,

Diminished, dissected,

Till she gave herself away,

Until nothing was left but a body—

Carrying his weight,

His rage, his fears.

Oh, my dear—

Wasn't she already dead?

I heard whispers about her-

SATISH PUTHRAN
SPEAKING SHADOWS
ECHOES FROM THE SILENT CORNERS

Words they would never let me hear.

Of the woman whose womb

Carried me for months,

Months not years,

Because she vanished and disappeared.

Yes,i was her abandoned child,

Cradled by a father,not a mother.

But how could a monster take her place?

And how could the stranger he married,

Ever make me feel safe?

I stumbled and fell,

As i tried to make my way,

Asking questions,lost in maze,

Disappeared in haze-

deciphering ,confused-

Why did this happen to me anyways?

SATISH PUTHRAN
SPEAKING SHADOWS
ECHOES FROM THE SILENT CORNERS

I no longer want this-not again.

For I was the woman in making,

Yet I could not relate

To the women who shaped me.

I could never be them.

What mother walks away

From a piece of herself?

And what woman stays,

Sacrificing her soul,

Her self-respect,

For the sake of them?

I had seen the extremes,

Yet I failed to comprehend—

How love and abuse

Could wear the same face,

Both masked in devotion.

But now as they speak to me,

As their stories become clear

Their voices grow louder.

They warn me—

Not to fall into the same trap.

To be young, independent,

A woman of my own.

Regret lingers in their eyes,

And their voices tremble,

Nevertheless, I hear them.

And,I promise and swear-

To be the glorious light of the dawn.

बुझा दिया उठे उस भूचाल को

साँसों के साथ एक भूचाल सा उठा था मन में,

विचार कुछ लेकर आया था संग अपने ,

कुछ बतलाना था उसे, कुछ समझना था उसे मुझे,

संग अपने वह मुझे उड़ा ना जाने किस दिशा ले चला।

खुद को संभालता हुआ मैं कुछ पूछ बैठे उससे हम,

उड़ा रहे संग अपने तुम, कहाँ ले जा रहे,

बतलाते क्यों ना कुछ तुम ?

सवाल जैसे मेरी भूचाल को शक्ति दे गई, वह उड़ती हुई मुझे छोड़ गई।

बीच मंझधार में फँसा , बिन माझी नाव सा मैं ,

कहीं किसी किनारे की तलाश में, स्थिरता की खोज में।

लगा सोचने मैं, इस भूचाल की कठोरता को, निर्दयता को ,
लगा निहारने मैं ,,,,

सहसा एक हवा उठी, जो छू मेरे मन को, शांत कर मन को,

भूचाल के नामोनिशान मिटाकर, मासूमियत के साथ लगी मुझे सहलाने।

मैं भी अपने सूखेपन को भुला,

संग उसके सवार लिया खुद को।

उसकी छाँव में, उसकी शीतलता में,

समा दिया खुद को,

बुझा दिया उठे उस भूचाल को,

बुझा दिया उठे उस भूचाल को ।

मुलाकात

आख़िरी मुलाकात, जी चलिए आज बात करते हैं मुलाकात पर।

नहीं जी, वो नहीं, जो आप समझ रहे हैं,

आमने-सामने मुलाकात की, नज़रों से देख सकें, ऐसी मुलाकात की,

उन्हें स्पर्श कर सकें, उस मुलाकात की।

जी, हम बात कर रहे हैं उस रूहानी मुलाकात की,

जो पत्र पढ़ते समय उसकी छवि से हुई थी,

जो उदास होने पर उनके बातों से हँसी आने पर हुई थी,

जो नींद से पहले आपकी आँखों में हुई थी,

जो आधी रात में आपके ख़याल में हुई थी।

जी हाँ, बात उस मुलाकात पर करते हैं–

कुछ कहते हैं, कुछ सुनते हैं, कुछ समझते हैं, कुछ लिख देते हैं,

तो कुछ उस मुलाकात के सहारे जीवन गुज़ार देते हैं।

वो चाँदनी रात में बैठे,

चाँद को निहारते-निहारते,

सपने उसकी मुलाकात के देखते।

चलती हुई हवा को ऐसे ही महसूस करते,

उसकी ठंडक से तुम सिहरते,

पर हवा के बहाव में उसे तलाशते,

उससे मिलने की सोचते।

यह मुलाकात ऐसी क्यों,

जो हर मुलाकात के बाद अगली मुलाकात का पता पूछते...?

© Dhananjay Gupta

चल कन्हैया

अंदर ही अंदर रो रहीं,

बाहर से मुस्कुराती राधा।

अंदर ही अंदर तड़प रहीं,

बाहर से मौन राधा।

पर करें भी क्या ? है विवश राधा।

सब कुछ त्याग दिया।

सिर्फ़ तेरा याद किया।

ओ कान्हा सुन!

आन पड़ी है बड़ी बाधा।

संकट में है तेरो राधा।

चल कन्हैया !

अब तनिक न देर कर ।

रो रहीं तोरी राधा।

चल कन्हैया !

आन पड़ी है बड़ी बाधा।

चल कन्हैया ! चल !

लिख दो जो जिए हो तुम उसके साथ

अब क्यों सोचते हो कि बात नहीं होती ?

हो गया जो होना था ।

अब क्यों रोते हो कि मुलाकात नहीं होती ?

हो गया यार जो होना था ।

जितना मिला वो भी तो कम नहीं था न यार

क्यों मायूस बैठे हो दोस्त

उठाओ अपनी तलवार

और चलो उस नदी के पास

लिख दो सब कुछ जो जिए हो तुम उसके साथ

चलो यार ! चलो यार !

लिख दो सब कुछ जो जिए हो तुम उसके साथ ।।

© Priyanshu Kumar

ECHOES OF YESTERDAY

When dry desolute darkness covers my mind in its humble shadows and I see nothing but my past disgrace, present suffering and vast nothingness beyond the horizon... I hope for a better start next time but the moment which is still makes me realize that what was the
beginning has passed away and what remains shall be long lasting in such a melancholic understanding I walk beyond the blue mountain down the steep passes and narrow valleys to discover what the future holds the blessings of light or hidden miseries is not my quest but I shall accept what comes forth.

एक रोज़ चांद को देखा

एक रोज़ मैंने चाँद को देखा,

चाँद की चाँदनी को देखा,

उसके चमक को देखा,

उसके भोलेपन को देखा,

उसकी मासूमियत को देखा।

और उसके उजाले को देखकर,

अपनी परछाईं को देखा।

चाँद सा गोल कुछ अपने सवाल को देखा।

उसके उजाले में मैंने अपने इतिहास को देखा।

समझ चाँद को रहे थे,

समझ खुद को बैठे।

एक रोज़ मैंने चाँद को देखा,

एक रोज़ मैंने चाँद को देखा ।

© Dhananjay Gupta

क्या है यह ,कुछ बतलाओ तो

क्या है ये, हाँ, वो जो तुम्हारी आँखों से?

बूँदें बनकर, तुम्हारे गालों को अपना रास्ता बना बहती जा रही हैं।

क्या है ये, जो आँखों से होकर तुम्हारे दिलों तक पहुँच रही हैं?

कुछ बतलाओ तो, कुछ समझाओ तो,

सिर्फ आँखों से बारिश की बूँदें गिराए जा रही हैं।

ये बूँदें सूखी भी नहीं कि,

फिर से बाढ़ आने के मौसम बनाए जा रही हैं,

क्या है ये, जो एक आँखों से दूसरी आँखों के सफ़र कर,

और प्रचंड हुए जा रही है?

रोको तो इन्हें, ज़रा बाँधो तो इन्हें,

किस जल्दी में हैं ये, कि सब बांध तोड़े जा रही हैं,

बिन कहे बहे जा रही हैं, कुछ बोझ तुम्हारा लिया जा रही हैं।

क्या है ये, जो आँखों से होकर मन को छूए जा रही हैं,

भटक रहे मन को शांत कर, दिलासा दिया जा रही हैं,

भरोसा बनकर कभी तोड़े भी जा रही हैं।

फिर से आ-आकर गले लगकर, फिर आँखों से विदा लिए,

बिना कुछ कहे, किसी दिशा में जाए जा रही हैं।

क्या है ये, जो आँखों से अपना रंग छुपाए जा रही हैं?

कौन है ये, जो आँखों को अपना हाल समझा ग़ायब हो रही हैं?

बिना नाम बताए, कहाँ ग़ायब हो जा रही हैं?

कौन है ये, आँखों से दुबारा मिलने का वादा करे जा रही हैं...?

© Dhananjay Gupta

A TALE WE WROTE TOGETHER

Hey! (with the intention of "तुम पढ़ लेना उन नज्मों को, जो किताबों से नहीं मेरी नजरों से बयां होंगी।")

And how it would be if we, on someday come across somewhere, where I or perhaps we, find our commonplace.

At the library!

Where, there will be long conversations, with the words of books and not ours. Where we would sing through eyes and hear through heart. With "सुर" in every breath and "लय" in every beat.

At a "public library" what we in general are supposed to be is in full silence. With just dumb reads in our mind, But there we will scream with joy, not apparently in a way that makes sound or disturbs others but sheer spiritually.

We'll thoroughly read what written in one another's eye with highlighting those- whose sound is way louder than the words that normally would have been spoken.

And what about songs? Some old/new romantics. Listening to it together and feeling it from the core of our heart, to murmuring together looking on eachother eyes and smiling with lips and teeth. That will match enough chords to bring up the 'urge' of a romantic song.

Now, don't tell me you are an 'earbuds' person where I still prefer 'wired earphones' over any others. Don't know why but, it is- what it is. It is what feels love to me when a same wire divides in two but still stays together. Picking up one earphone for me, another for you and we know, these "one and another" is still one. Here is what I believe that would also give us the feeling of "us".

Then, being in library when you'll pick your favourite book from amongst the favourites there will be a scent of me in every book ,in every page, in every line, and in every word, Since it was 'I' who have already read your all favourite books so that I never left behind being your favourite.

And then after finishing that book together, moving towards the roof, I'll even tell you the stories that you might not have read anywhere in your favourite and not so favourite books. Since, the writer has not written any book yet, 'बेशक' I'm talking about my own stories.

There also would be some known tales of some mythological characters whose stories are worth telling and worth to be heard that I'll tell you, But the sheer difference would be the way I will recite them, and the way you'll hear it.

What we generally call it mythology, is not actually, if we believe in it. And I'll make you believe in the tales of itihasa and not mythology.

I will confirm to you my belief in it and eventually you will fall in love with it.

I will tell you the tales of stars- Arundhati & Vashishtha (Mizar & Alcor) and Dhruvtara (polaris/pole star). which have been wonderfully woven in the folktales, such as how they once existed in flash and blood and how and why we know them in stars. I will unwove it one by one for you and tell you what significance they hold within our 'rich culture' and far.

And when my stories will going to wave an end, you will further add to my stories, to form a beautiful ending to every melancholy. And then you will realise why I call you my co-writer. Since it's the ending that decides if the story was worth listening/reading or not. So with life. And So with us.

And with that-

/ हर लफ्ज़ जब सिमटेगा गा

फिर दिल की आंखों से गुफ्तगू होंगी।

की, किताबों से पढ़ लिए बातें- गैरों के दिलो की

जब बात अपनी होगी तो केवल नजरे गवाह होंगी। /

© Komal Gupta

WHISPERS OF THE SHORE

At the flawless sea shore
Let me stay a wholly more.
Wanna stare the endless - horizon
To find nothing but peace of my version.
From the movement of fishes at lone,
I want to feel even the vibration of a single stone.
From my-top to my-toe
Surely, the breezes will overflow.
In a wide - open eyesight,
I'll feel the scenario at a level of paradise.
When the day will come close to an end,
I'll set a runway for the night for land.
I'll sing an "ode" with the stars for the half-moon,
In order to get the attention, at least a half of spoon.

© Komal Gupta

ना भुलाने वाली मौत

तेरे इश्क़ में हमने भी अपने दिल को जलाया है,

महसूस हुआ ना तुझे यह तूने कैसा नसीब पाया है ।

भुला दू तो ज़िन्दगी पा जाऊं,

ना भुलाने वाली मौत को हमने गले लगाया है ।

रोज जलूँगा तेरे लिए कभी चाहना तो मेरी आह सुन्ना,

हो सके तो देना एक पत्थर उछाल, चोट लगे तो भुला दू तेरे ख्याल ।

उस पत्थर की चोट से मैंने खुदको पाया है,

ना भुलाने वाली मौत को हमने गले लगाया है ।

धड़कन चुबती दिल को हमारे, साँसे नसों को करती तार तार,

धड़कने हमारी कराती पल-पल मृत्यु का दीदार ।

रूह को चढ़ा ताप है, ह्रदय ने हमारे यह अभिशाप पाया है,

ना भुलाने वाली मौत को हमने गले लगाया है ।

कोई पूछे तो बताए

कोई पूछे तो बताए की,

देखा है हमने चाँद तोड़कर लाने वालो को सीपियों का घर तोड़ते,

देखा है हमने तारे तोड़कर लाने वालो को दिल के टुकड़े समेटते,

देखा है हमने प्रेम विवाह करने वालो को खुदके घर को तोड़ते,

सुना है अधजन्मे बच्चो को जोड़े प्रेम की बलि चढ़ाते हैं,

मन भरजाता प्रेम से तो रास्ते अलग कर जाते हैं।

कोई पूछे तो बताए की,

सुना है जिस्म का मोह भी प्रेम का दर्शन कहलाता है,

नज़रो की बातों को ज़माने में अनदेखा कर दिया जाता है,

देखा है हमने साथ के लिए प्रेमियों को तड़पते,

देखा है मोह भंग के बाद अपने रास्ते सरकते ।

कोई पूछे तो बताए की,

अनजाना प्रेम बड़ा निर्बल है,पराये के स्पर्श से होता अधिक दुर्बल है,

संग हाँथ पकड़कर राहों में चलने वाले कमरे में अपने खो जाते हैं,

प्रेम मर जाता है परिंदे पिंजरे में रह जाते हैं,

देखा है हमने प्रेमी पर हाँथ उठाते उसको, निर्दयता की मूरत मानव बनने आज चला है,

प्रेम के ऐसे रूप का अभी हमे पता चला है ।

कोई पूछे तो बताए की,

डर लगता प्रेम से हमको,क्या हो अगर मै कर लू मगर ना हो कभी उसको,

जीवन सवरता देखा नहीं, जुदाई की कथा हमने जानी है,

राधा कृष्णा के दर्द को हमने प्रेम की कला मानी है ।

जुदाई, आंसू, व्यथा, आकर्षण अगर प्रेम से जन्मे हैं,

तो क्या हम सही नहीं कहते मृत्यु प्रेम की संरचना,मोह तो जंजाल है,

प्रेम -मोह के चक्रव्यूह में फसा जीवन का काल है,

समय बड़ा विकराल है, दुनिया मोह का जाल है ।

प्रेम अदृस्य है, शायद मुक्ति का इकलौता मार्ग है,

हां प्रेम मुक्ति का मार्ग है, मोह जीवन चक्र की उलझन ।

© Adarsh Anand

ABOUT THE AUTHOR

SATISH PUTHRAN
SPEAKING SHADOWS
ECHOES FROM THE SILENT CORNERS

SATISH PUTHRAN

INDIA AUTHORS ACADEMY : IAA AUTHOR AWARDEE 2024

SATISH PUTHRAN
SPEAKING SHADOWS
ECHOES FROM THE SILENT CORNERS

Satish Puthran, born in Mangaluru, Karnataka on 08th October 1984 (Indian Air Force Day), was brought up in Bombay (Mumbai), Maharashtra. An animal lover and travel enthusiast by nature.

He is an alumnus of St. Mary's High School, Dahisar East, Mumbai : 1999-2000 batch. He has received the Best Student Of The Year award at St. Lawrence High School, Avdhoot Nagar, Dahisar East, Mumbai for the year 1991-1992.

He holds a Diploma in International Airlines, Travel, and Tourism Management with AMADEUS as the computer reservation system. He was a National Service Scheme (N.S.S) volunteer for 2 years under the University of Mumbai and completed the Civil Defence Academy (Basic & Warden Service Course) in Maharashtra. He is a professional marathon runner who can give tough competition to anyone.

He has participated in the Mumbai Ultra 12 Hour Run 2017 held on 13th August 2017, covering a distance of 55K without any prior practice. He has volunteered for many marathon events, including participation since 1st November 2015 (Karnataka Rajyotsava) at Central Park, Kharghar, Navi Mumbai for Mastek Foundation Run 2015 : 5K in 00:39:41.

He has participated in the Manipal Marathon 2019 in the 21K category, Manipal, Mangaluru, Karnataka (National

Level) in February 2019, and broke his 21K timing at PKDM 2019 in March 2019.

He has volunteered with the Bhumi Mumbai NGO for many years and participated in various activities. He was involved in the Bhumi Nakshatra Sports event held at HP Nagar, Chembur, with Bosco Boys Home, Borivali West, Mumbai, Maharashtra, where he served as Shelter Home Manager for orphanage kids.

He was a Judge and Guest of Honour for Ghe Bharari presents 'Bal Mahotsav 2023 and Bal Mahotsav 2024, annual sports events for underprivileged kids held at Dr. M. G. Parulekar School, Vasai West.

Tour Guide with 'DK's Yatra Unlimited Holidays' for 'Mumbai (Dadar - Naigaon) - Trimbakeshwar - Shirdi - Shani Shingnapur' in March 2024 with '108' senior citizens onboard.

Currently co-author of two anthologies published by Thoughts Hymn Publishers, Noida, Uttar Pradesh, India. The anthologies are titled The Aurora's Embrace Volume 4 and Velvet Shadows Volume 1.

Received 1st Prize in Poetry Writing Competition held on Sunday, 18th August 2024 at Pejawara Mutt, Prabhat Colony, Santacruz East, Mumbai during 70th Annual General Body Meeting of Saphalya Seva Sangha, Mumbai.

'Gauravarpane 2025' At '84th Saphalya Seva Sangha, Mumbai Annual Day Celebration' At 'Buntara Bhavana, Kurla East' On '05.01.2025'.

Dreams Take Flight: The Girl Who Dared Available On :

E-Book Hindi (amazon.in) :

https://amzn.in/d/0yFmK5N

E-Book English (amazon.in) :

https://amzn.in/d/06Y3g16

E-Book English (amazon.in) :

https://amzn.in/d/06Y3g16

Paperback (pothi.com) :

https://store.pothi.com/book/satish-puthran-dreams-take-flight/

E-Book Hindi (pothi.com) :

https://store.pothi.com/book/ebook-satish-puthran-dreams-take-flight-0/

E-Book English (pothi.com) :

https://store.pothi.com/book/ebook-satish-puthran-dreams-take-flight/

INTERNATIONAL READERS :

E-Book Hindi (amazon.com) : https://a.co/d/90tAa06

E-Book English (amazon.com) : https://a.co/d/2skaBkz

Paperback (amazon.com) : https://a.co/d/9NgvXne

FEEDBACK (AUTHOR SATISH PUTHRAN)

FOLLOW ME ON

INSTAGRAM

SATISH PUTHRAN

https://www.instagram.com/08_satish_iaf

EMERGING AUTHOR

https://www.instagram.com/emerging_author_iaf

TELEGRAM

https://t.me/satish_08_iaf_iaa

TWITTER (X)

https://www.x.com/satishindianiaf

EMAIL

emerging_author_iaf@yahoo.com

EPILOGUE

SATISH PUTHRAN
SPEAKING SHADOWS
ECHOES FROM THE SILENT CORNERS

This beautiful poem is heartfelt dedication to all the contributors & co-authors of 'Speaking Shadows: Echoes from the Silent Corners'

आपकी रचनाएँ और योगदान इस कविता के सार को जीवित करती हैं। आप सभी उन फरिश्तों की तरह हैं, जिन्होंने अपने शब्दों से सन्नाटों को आवाज़ दी और सन्नाटों के बीच प्रेम का संदेश फैलाया।

I, Author Satish Puthran beautifully acknowledge their work and contribution while celebrating the love and collaboration behind the anthology.

प्यार के फरिश्ते

कुछ फरिश्ते भगवान बन जाते हैं,

कुछ फरिश्ते इंसान बन जाते हैं,

जो दूसरों को दिल से प्यार करें,

वो प्यार के फरिश्ते बन जाते हैं।

AFTERWORD

SATISH PUTHRAN
SPEAKING SHADOWS
ECHOES FROM THE SILENT CORNERS

As we come to the close of this anthology, Speaking Shadows: Echoes from the Silent Corners, I am filled with gratitude and admiration for the talented authors who have contributed their voices, thoughts, and emotions to this collection. Each piece in this book is a reflection of the unique perspectives, experiences, and creativity that have come together in this collaborative journey.

This anthology is more than just a collection of words—it's a testament to the power of shared experiences, the beauty of storytelling, and the unspoken connection between us all. It is a celebration of the silent corners where our stories reside, waiting to be heard.

I want to extend my heartfelt thanks to every contributing author for their dedication and passion. Your words have not only enriched this anthology but have also given it life, and for that, I am truly honored.
Together, we have created something beautiful—a work that echoes the stories of our hearts, our minds, and our spirits.

May this anthology continue to inspire, provoke thought, and resonate with all those who read it. And may the love and collaboration behind it always remind us of the power we hold when we come together to share our voices.

www.ingramcontent.com/pod-product-compliance
Ingram Content Group UK Ltd.
Pitfield, Milton Keynes, MK11 3LW, UK
UKHW020050200726
13845UKWH00055B/630

9 789334 265309